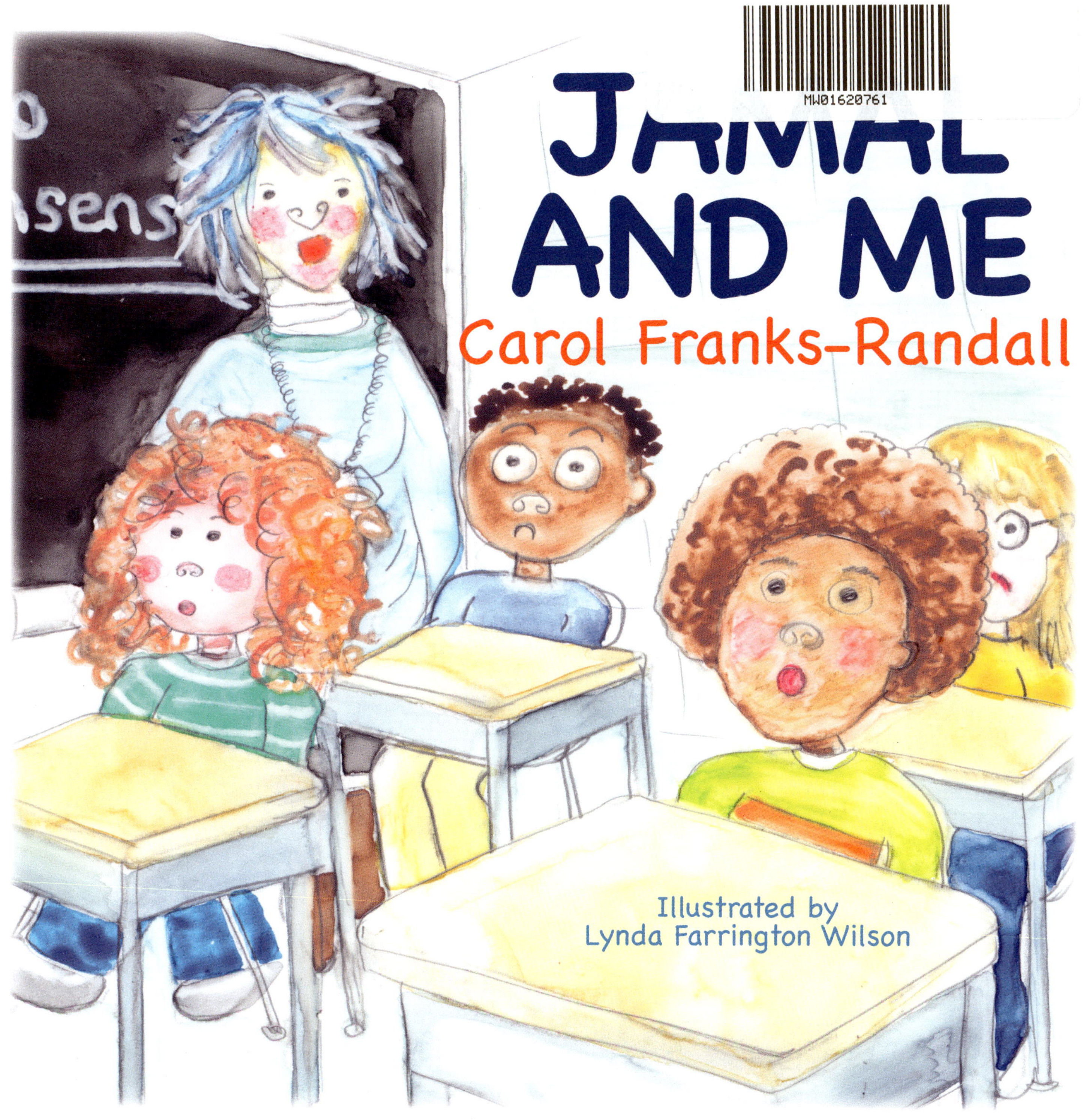
JAMAL
AND ME
Carol Franks-Randall
Illustrated by
Lynda Farrington Wilson

JAMAL AND ME

https://carolfranksrandall.com

Illustrated by Lynda Farrington Wilson

www.lyndafarringtonwilson.com

Browns Corner Press

ISBN-13:978-0999399705

ISBN-10: 0999399705

This book is dedicated to my grandchildren:
Zoë, Tyler, Elle, Gabrielle, Lila, and Theodore;
to educators everywhere,

and

to my husband Robert who has inspired me to
pursue my hopes and dreams.

January 2018

Dear Sarah –
I hope you enjoy this book!
I hope Book Birdie continues to
thrive in 2018!

All the best –
[illegible]

Jamal's family moved from the city to a small town in the suburbs. He did not know anyone and felt lonely and out of place. There were very few sidewalks, no streetlights and lots of grass and trees.

Jamal had to start third grade in a new school. On the first day of school, he met his teacher, Miss Iceburg. Miss Iceburg was very strict. "I tolerate no nonsense in my classroom!" she told her students in a loud, stern voice.

No
Nonsens

Jamal had a rough start to the school year. On the school bus he pushed students out of their seats and called them unmentionable names. The other children did not like him.

EXIT
Get out of my way!! I want to sit there!

Jamal threw food in the cafeteria and made fun of his classmates on the playground.

Nobody wanted to be his friend.

Whenever Miss Iceburg spoke to Jamal about his behavior, he mimicked her and rolled his eyes. Jamal even told Miss Iceburg he was going to get her fired.

Jamal

Dr. Toughlove, I have never met a child like Jamal. He is ruining my class and I won't have it! I want him removed!

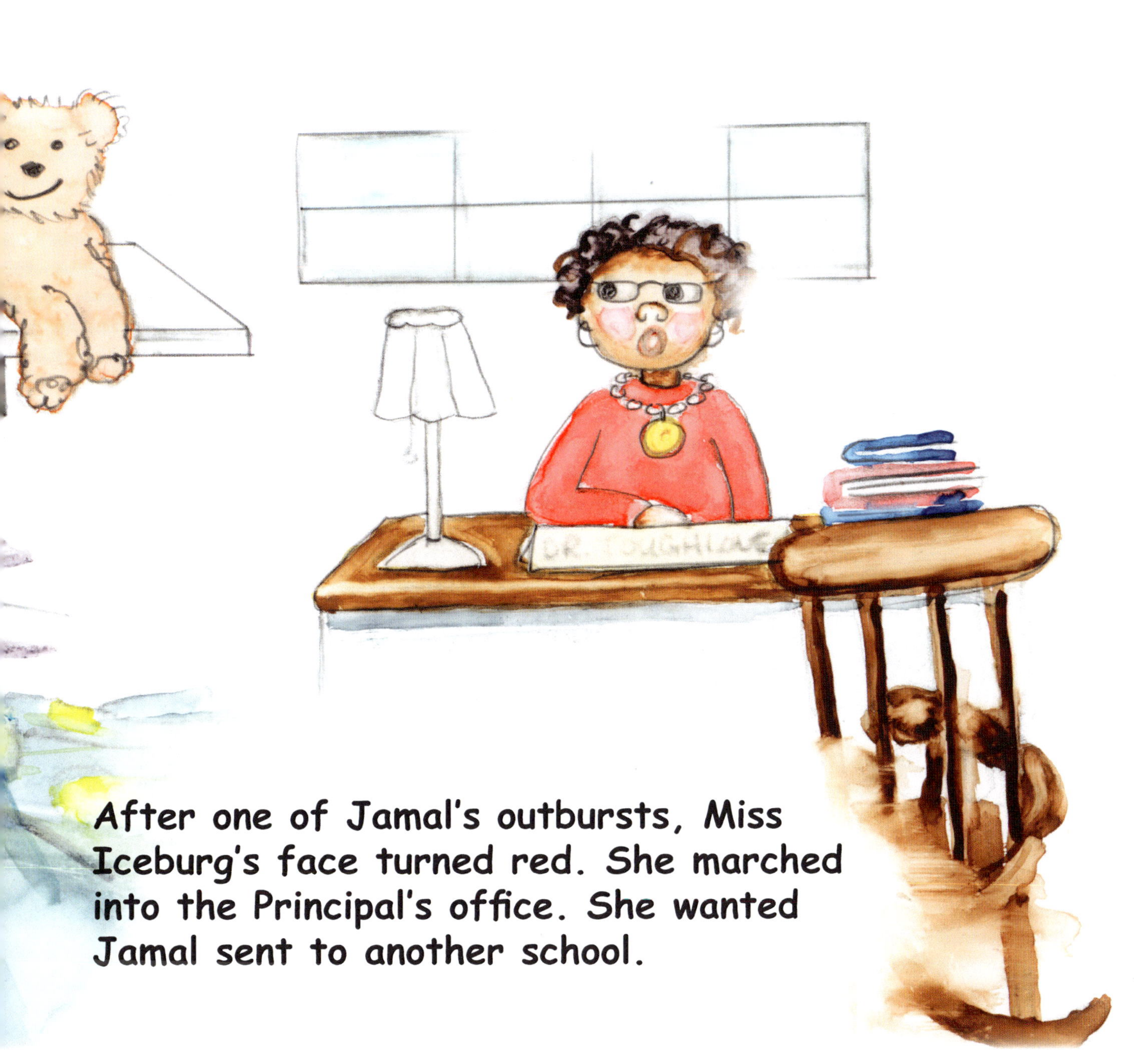

After one of Jamal's outbursts, Miss Iceburg's face turned red. She marched into the Principal's office. She wanted Jamal sent to another school.

Instead of sending Jamal to another school, Miss Iceburg sent him to the Principal's office when he misbehaved. Dr. Toughlove told him she liked him, but didn't like his behavior when he was unkind or disrespectful.

Whenever Dr. Toughlove asked Jamal if he had done something naughty he always admitted it.

Did you yell at Miss Iceburg and tell her she can't tell you what to do?
Yes I did.
DR. TOUGHLOVE

Dr. Toughlove had a long talk with Jamal about rolling his eyes at his teacher. While Jamal was talking to Dr. Toughlove, she rolled her eyes. "Did you like it when I rolled my eyes while you were talking?" Jamal had to admit he didn't like it one bit.

"It is important to treat everyone with respect," said Dr. Toughlove.

TOUGHLOVE

Dr. Toughlove and Miss Iceburg continued to talk to each other about Jamal's behavior. They agreed that when Jamal behaved well, Miss Iceburg would praise him for his appropriate behavior and send him to the Principal's office to tell Dr. Toughlove.

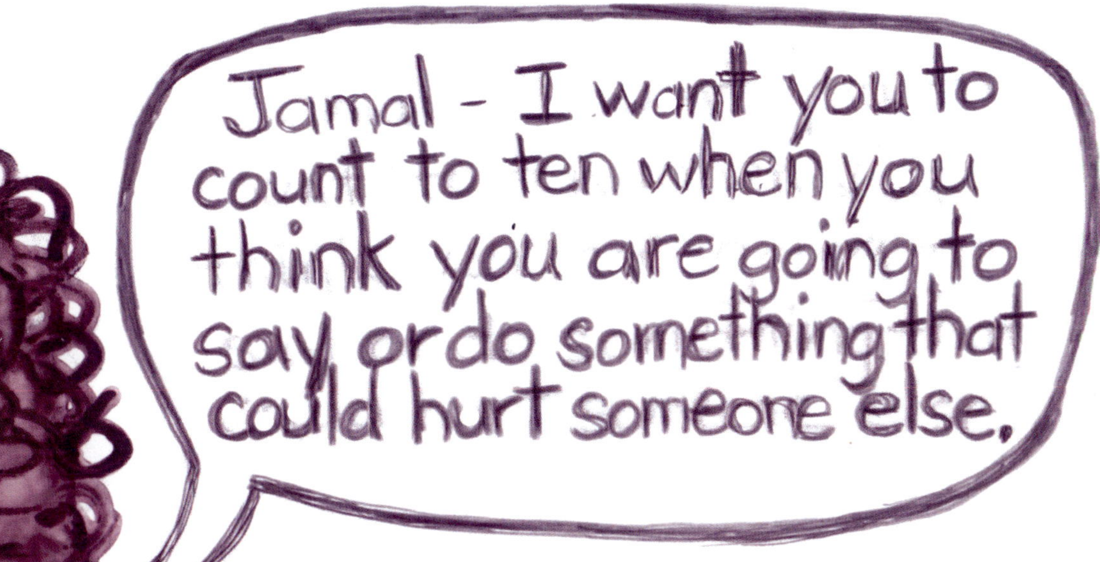

If Jamal forgot to behave appropriately, Dr. Toughlove reminded him to think before he acts and make good choices. She told him she knew he could get along with his classmates and teachers. Whenever she could, Dr. Toughlove told him that she believed in him.

Dr. Toughlove and Jamal made a pact that if they saw each other in the hallway they would give each other the "thumbs up" sign. Jamal knew Dr. Toughlove was his special friend and she liked him.

Miss Iceburg noticed that Jamal began to be nicer to his classmates, and they in turn were nicer to him. He was sent to the Principal's office more often for making good choices than for misbehaving.

At the end of the school year there was an assembly. Students in each grade were given special awards. All of the children came to the auditorium to hear the names announced. They were very excited!

AWARDS

Miss Iceburg said, "The award for the most improved student in the third grade goes to..........."

Jamal!

Dr. Toughlove was on the stage and she gave Jamal a big hug. She told him she was proud of him.

AWARDS
MOST IMPROVED

On the last day of school, after all of the children left for summer vacation, Dr. Toughlove was emptying her mailbox. There was an envelope addressed to her.

Dr. Toughlove

SMITH
JONES
Dr. Toughlove
TOUGHLOVE

Dr. Toughlove's face broke out in a big smile. She put Jamal's letter on the wall in her office.

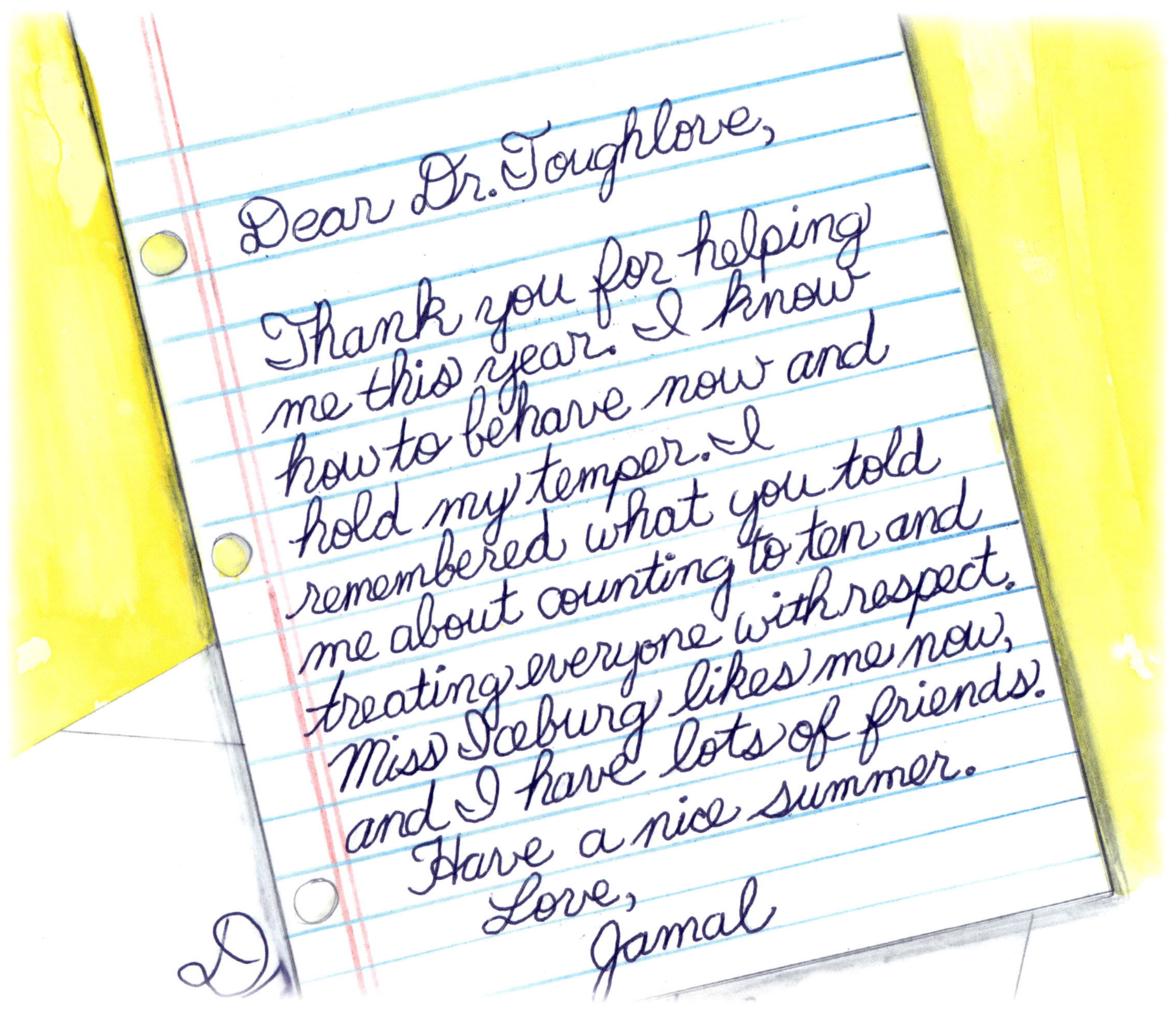

Dear Dr. Toughlove,

Thank you for helping me this year. I know how to behave now and hold my temper. I remembered what you told me about counting to ten and treating everyone with respect. Miss Iceburg likes me now, and I have lots of friends.

Have a nice summer.

Love,

Jamal

What a treat! I get to read Jamal's letter every day!
Love Jamal
DR. TOUGHLOVE

ABOUT THE AUTHOR

Carol Franks-Randall, EdD, began her career as a special education teacher and worked as a school administrator and college instructor in New York State. After retirement she and her husband Robert moved to Maryland's Eastern Shore. She keeps busy with photography, travel, crocheting, volunteering in her community and spending time with her children and grandchildren. JAMAL AND ME is her first book.

Visit her at https://carolfranksrandall.com

ABOUT THE ILLUSTRATOR

Lynda Farrington Wilson is an award-winning author and illustrator. She loves to interpret manuscripts into the whimsical world of color, texture and the unexpected detail in the Lime Crab Cottage, her North Carolina studio. Lynda's passion is in creating books to raise awareness for children with special needs, as the youngest of her three sons has autism.

Visit her at www.lyndafarringtonwilson.com

Jamal

81589368R00022

Made in the USA
Columbia, SC
27 November 2017